MIGHTY MACHINES IN ACTION

Race Cars

by Chris Bowman

BELLWETHER MEDIA • MINNEAPOLIS, MN

Note to Librarians, Teachers, and Parents:

Blastoff! Readers are carefully developed by literacy experts and combine standards-based content with developmentally appropriate text.

Level 1 provides the most support through repetition of high-frequency words, light text, predictable sentence patterns, and strong visual support.

Level 2 offers early readers a bit more challenge through varied simple sentences, increased text load, and less repetition of high-frequency words.

Level 3 advances early-fluent readers toward fluency through increased text and concept load, less reliance on visuals, longer sentences, and more literary language.

Level 4 builds reading stamina by providing more text per page, increased use of punctuation, greater variation in sentence patterns, and increasingly challenging vocabulary.

Level 5 encourages children to move from "learning to read" to "reading to learn" by providing even more text, varied writing styles, and less familiar topics.

Whichever book is right for your reader, Blastoff! Readers are the perfect books to build confidence and encourage a love of reading that will last a lifetime!

This edition first published in 2018 by Bellwether Media, Inc.

No part of this publication may be reproduced in whole or in part without written permission of the publisher. For information regarding permission, write to Bellwether Media, Inc., Attention: Permissions Department, 5357 Penn Avenue South, Minneapolis, MN 55419.

Library of Congress Cataloging-in-Publication Data

Names: Bowman, Chris, 1990- author.
Title: Race Cars / by Chris Bowman.
Description: Minneapolis, MN : Bellwether Media, Inc., 2018. | Series: Blastoff! Readers: Mighty Machines in Action | Includes bibliographical references and index. | Audience: Ages 5-8. | Audience: K to Grade 3.
Identifiers: LCCN 2017031303 (print) | LCCN 2017032237 (ebook) | ISBN 9781626177598 (hardcover : alk. paper) | ISBN 9781681034645 (ebook)
Subjects: LCSH: Automobiles, Racing–Juvenile literature.
Classification: LCC TL236 (ebook) | LCC TL236 .B69 2018 (print) | DDC 629.228/5–dc23
LC record available at https://lccn.loc.gov/2017031303

Editor: Rebecca Sabelko   Designer: Steve Porter

Printed in the United States of America, North Mankato, MN.

Table of Contents

A Close Race   4
Need for Speed   8
Bodies, Engines, and Tires   12
Fan Favorites   20
Glossary   22
To Learn More   23
Index   24

A CLOSE RACE

The race cars are lined up and ready to go. Engines **rev** as the green flag drops.

The cars speed across the
starting line. The race is on!

Soon, the white flag waves.
There is only one lap left!

One car pulls ahead. It crosses
the finish line first. What a race!

asphalt

Race cars are vehicles built for speed. Some drive on **asphalt**.

Many speed on road **courses** or around oval racetracks.

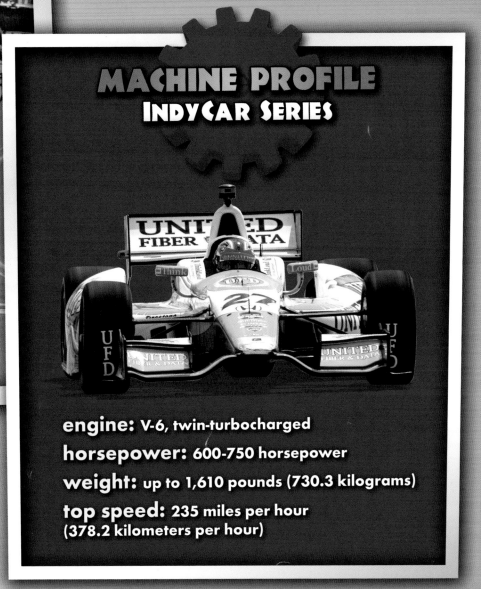

MACHINE PROFILE
IndyCar Series

engine: V-6, twin-turbocharged

horsepower: 600-750 horsepower

weight: up to 1,610 pounds (730.3 kilograms)

top speed: 235 miles per hour (378.2 kilometers per hour)

Other cars are built to race around dirt tracks or speed down winding trails.

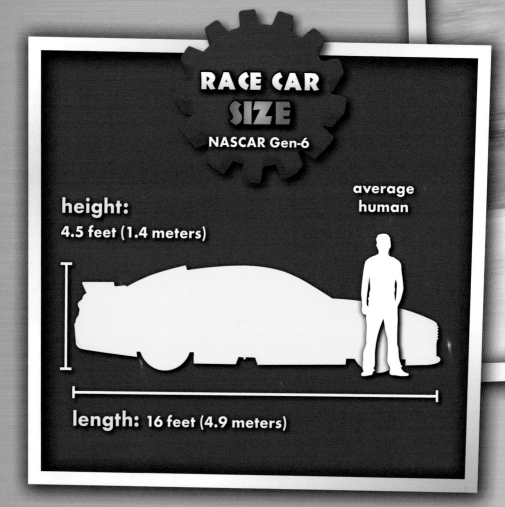

RACE CAR SIZE
NASCAR Gen-6

height:
4.5 feet (1.4 meters)

average human

length: 16 feet (4.9 meters)

Sometimes these courses mix asphalt and dirt!

BODIES, ENGINES, AND TIRES

Race car bodies have many shapes. But they are all made for speed.

Indy car

stock car

Stock cars look like regular cars. **Indy cars** have **aerodynamic** shapes.

engine

drag racing car

Powerful engines move race cars around the track.

Some cars reach speeds of over 200 miles (322 kilometers) per hour!

COMMON
RACE CARS

rally car

Formula 1 car

Indy car

stock car

Thick, wide tires help race cars **grip** the track.

tire

The tires get worn down at
high speeds. They are often
changed during the race!

harness

Driving at high speeds can be dangerous. **Harnesses** keep race car drivers safe.

Roll cages are there to protect the drivers if they crash.

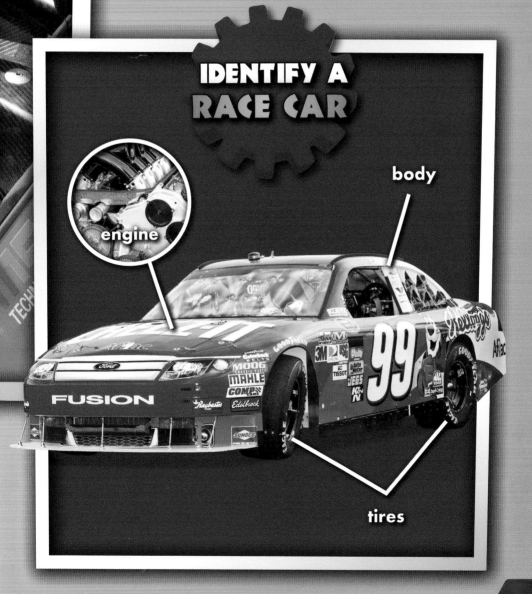

IDENTIFY A
RACE CAR

engine

body

tires

FAN FAVORITES

There are many racing fans around the world. They cheer for their favorite drivers.

With so many types of cars,
there is a race for everyone!

Glossary

aerodynamic—having a shape that can move through the air quickly

asphalt—a material used to make roads

courses—places where races are held

grip—to hold tight

harnesses—sets of straps that keep drivers safe

Indy cars—single-seat racing cars with the engines in the rear

rev—to turn a part of the engine; the engine makes a noise when it revs.

roll cages—steel frames inside race cars that keep drivers safe if the cars roll over

stock cars—cars used for racing that are similar to cars normally driven by the public; stock cars have more powerful engines than regular cars.

To Learn More

AT THE LIBRARY

Kortemeier, Todd. *Superstars of NASCAR*. Mankato, Minn.: Amicus High Interest, Amicus Ink, 2017.

Silverman, Buffy. *How Do Formula One Race Cars Work?* Minneapolis, Minn.: Lerner Publications, 2016.

West, David. *Race Cars*. Mankato, Minn.: Smart Apple Media, 2017.

ON THE WEB

Learning more about race cars is as easy as 1, 2, 3.

1. Go to www.factsurfer.com.

2. Enter "race cars" into the search box.

3. Click the "Surf" button and you will see a list of related web sites.

With factsurfer.com, finding more information is just a click away.

Index

aerodynamic, 13

asphalt, 8, 11

bodies, 12, 19

courses, 9, 11

crash, 19

drag racing car, 14

drive, 8, 18

drivers, 18, 19, 20

engines, 4, 9, 14, 19

fans, 20

Formula 1 car, 15

harnesses, 18

Indy car, 9, 12, 13, 15

race, 5, 7, 10, 17, 21

rally car, 15

rev, 4

roll cages, 19

shapes, 12, 13

size, 9, 10

speed, 5, 8, 9, 10, 12, 15, 17, 18

stock cars, 13, 15

tires, 16, 17, 19

tracks, 9, 10, 14, 16

trails, 10

types, 15, 21

The images in this book are reproduced through the courtesy of: Natursports, front cover; MAX ROSSI/ Newscom, pp. 4-5, 6-7; Michael Alesi/ Newscom, p. 4; Walter Arce, pp. 8-9, 17; HodagMedia, pp. 9, 12-13, 15 (bottom left); Montypeter, pp. 10-11; Ron Niebrugge/ Alamy, p. 13; rcyoung, pp. 14-15; Lawrence Weslowski Jr, p. 15 (bottom right),19; David Acosta Allely, p. 15 (top right); CHEN WS, p. 15 (top left); cristiano barni, pp. 16-17; Alvey & Towers Picture Library/ Alamy, pp. 18-19; Yuen Man Cheung/ Alamy, p. 19; Daniel Hurlimann, pp. 20-21.